The Way Out Is Through

Feelings Surrounding Loss, Grief, and Heartbreak

Erin Baker

Made with ❤ on the BookLeaf Publishing Platform
www.bookleafpub.in
www.bookleafpub.com

Dedication

For all the broken hearts
You are not alone

For everyone caring for a broken heart:
You are appreciated

Preface

In this collection you will find many types and degrees of heartbreak, and a multitude of emotions and feelings surrounding each. While we are all unique, the human experiences of loss, grief, and heartbreak are not. Writing this collection of poems was a challenge because I had to revisit not only my own pain, grief, and loss, but also that of my loved ones.

You gotta resurrect the deep pain within you
and give it a place to live that's not within your body.
Let it live in art.
Let it live in writing.
Let it live in music.
Let it be devoured by building brighter connections.
Your body is not a coffin for pain to be buried in.
Put it somewhere else.
-Ehime Ora

If you find yourself, or someone you love, reflected in these words, I hope you will feel a sense of comfort knowing you're not alone in the trenches. It's difficult to let the world see your raw edges, but I choose to let my pain live in writing. I hope you, too, find a place to let your pain live.

Acknowledgements

Thank you for believing in me when no one else did,
not even myself.
TTG

Unanswered

"Don't," I whispered to the empty room,
To no one but the universe itself.
The universe didn't care,
And carried on destroying me.

"Why?" I asked the darkened closet,
Where only ghosts could hear me cry.
The ghosts might have cared,
But have no power over the ways of the world.

"No," I pleaded with the night,
From the floor so cold and unyielding
The night can't care,
And continued to pass by slowly.

"Stop," I begged from my lonely bed,
To my heart who was endlessly breaking.
My heart did care,
But had to break to build a new me.

Without

I have to find a way
A way to live without.
Without your sunshine and your tears
Without your laughter and your rainclouds

I have to find a way
A way to breathe without.
Without the warmth you shared
Without the happiness you brought

I have to find a way
A way to be without.
Without your hopes and dreams and fears
Without your joy and hugs

How can I find a way
A way to exist without?
Without your love
Is there any way to exist at all?

I have to find a way
A way to smile without.
Without your presence here
Without your curiosity and strength

I have to find a way
A way to be happy without.
Without your face
Without your friendship

I have to find a way
A way to move on without.
Without your belief in me
Without even hearing your voice

I have to find a way.

A way

Without

Stay

It hit me like a sucker punch
When they told me you were gone
Though I could clearly see the evidence
I was desperately holding on

This feeling in my gut
Like something had been removed
The utter lack of control
Left my mind and spirit bruised

How could you be gone
When yesterday you were here?
Disbelief clouds my mind
My heart consumed with fear

I hurt so much I can barely move
Can't even muster the strength to cry
No shoulder to lean on
Would anyone care if I die?

"Nothing to do now,
These things, they can't be changed.
Time to put your brave face on."
My frown has to be rearranged

"Don't talk about your grief,
It makes people feel uneasy.
Just find a distraction, you'll get over it."
The thought makes me feel queasy.

"It's uncomfortable to be around you,
People don't know what to say."
But I don't need words from anyone
I just need someone to stay.

Murky

How do you find the path forward
When nothing is at all clear
How can you put one foot in front of the other
When you can't see the terrain

How do you love again
When your heart hurts with every breath
How does the next day come
When your world has ended

How is it that no one knows what to do
When everyone wants to help
How do you explain it to them
When you barely have the energy to think

How can those who love you ignore you
When you need them the most
How can friends turn their backs on you
When your face is swollen from tears

How do you trust them again
When they weren't there for you
How do you trust anyone
When they say "isn't time to move on?"

How do you hide your pain
When it eats away at your very core
How do you focus on conversations
When all you can hear is your heart breaking

How can you care for others
When you don't care about anything at all
How do you go on living
When you're crushed by the weight of loss.

How do you open your eyes
When you'll never see your person again
How do you breathe
When the air is so murky

Hollow

He brought me home,
I sat on the couch
After we got the news

He treated me gently,
I stared into space
After we got the news

He ordered us lunch,
I ate it, I guess
After we got the news

He talked to me softly,
I couldn't move
After we got the news

He picked up our toddler,
I felt nothing
After we got the news

He tucked me in and held me,
I turned away and lie awake
After we got the news

He didn't understand,
I couldn't explain
After we got the news

He grew impatient,
I was empty inside
After we got the news

He was hurting too,
I didn't realize
After we got the news

He carried on,
I went through the motions
After we got the news

He soon smiled and laughed,
I was a shell of a person
After we got the news

He turned to someone else
I was left with nothing
After we got the news

Lost

You were not all I lost

I also lost the opportunity to meet you
To see your face after months of wondering what you
would look like

To watch you grow
To learn with you what you like and dislike

To hold your hand
To stand proudly while you graduate

To hug you in moments happy and sad
To soothe your fears

To cheer as you take your first steps
To listen to you laugh

To witness the pain when your best wasn't good enough
To hear your first word

To wipe your tears
To help you through your first heartbreak

To see you realize you can do hard things
To whisper "that's my baby" when you turn 18, 21, 35, 40

To dance with you in the rain, or on your wedding day
To make snow angels with you

To pour the bubbles into your bath
To hang your art up on the fridge

To show you how to let go, the way I have to now

You were not all I lost

Alone

It's breathtakingly lonely
-----Here in the sea of loss
You have only you
And a small raft
-----Friends come by
Some in canoes
Some on yachts
-----They call out to you
They wish you well
And send their love
-----But they can't join you
They don't think about
The havoc of their wake
-----Now once again you're alone
Just you and your thoughts
No one seems to notice
-----Your raft is breaking down
You have no where to turn
No one around to help
-----You haven't learned to swim
Your life vest is gone
And you don't know how to navigate
-----Which is why you're stranded here in the first place
Because everyone else moved forward

And no one showed you the map

-----You try to call out

But your voice can't be heard

Over the sounds of their happy milestones

-----Some hear the call but won't answer

Because you've been stuck too long

They don't think you're trying hard enough

-----They're afraid you'll only bring them down

If they get too close

Your grief might rub off on them

-----So you have to figure it out yourself

It hasn't worked so far

But maybe some solution will come to you

-----Before you drown

Alone

-----Here in the sea of loss

Betrayal

You learn that you should love yourself
From a pretty early age,
But then your body betrays you
And you're filled with self-loathing and rage.
It's technically what your body was intended to do,
If it can't even do that,
What good is it?

Your coworkers avert their eyes,
They don't want to acknowledge your pain.
This is a workplace, after all.
"Put her out of our misery, it would be more humane!"
Betrayed by the whispers you pretend not to hear,
Rooms that go silent when you enter.
No chance you'll get that promotion now that you're
"distracted".

If that weren't enough,
You feel betrayed by God.
How could He let this happen?
How could He leave your heart feeling so clawed?
Teenagers have babies every day,
Babies they don't even want, don't even love,
He can't spare one baby for you?

And it doesn't stop there, oh no.
When friends don't acknowledge t what you're going
through,
It feels like a massive betrayal - these are your friends!
Maybe they do care, but they don't know what to say or
do.
They don't want to upset you with their happy lives
And they don't know how to help you,
So they just avoid you.

The hits keep coming
When your family never speaks of it
Trust betrayed when they roll their eyes at your tears.
Like this should be your shameful secret.
You should really move on,
Being sad won't bring your baby back,
You need to get over it.

But the worst thing of all?
It doesn't hurt less because you've done it before
You never get used to it
In fact, each time hurts more.
The ultimate betrayal comes when your body does it
again.
And again. And again. And again.

Numb

I should be in disbelief, I should feel angry
I should be inconsolable, I should feel dejected
I should be sad, I should feel the weight of this loss
I should be willing to exchange anything
For one more day, one more year
I should feel devastated, I should be quiet
I should feel despair, I should be crying
I should feel like crawling into a hole,
And never coming out
I should be in denial, I should feel melancholy
I should be mournful, I should feel sorrow
I should be depressed, I should feel something

But I don't
And I'm not.

So why don't I feel guilty?

Schoolyard

They say First Is The Worst
But I don't think that's true.
You've never felt this loss, this pain, this heartache
before
Because it's the first
And maybe for some, it is the worst
Because it's the only.

They say Second Is The Best
But let's be real,
There is no "best" in this scenario.
You've gone through it before but it never gets any easier
You don't know what to expect,
Because no two heartbreaks are the same.

They say Third Is The Nerd With The Hairy Chest
But obviously that can't be right,
Or you wouldn't be here. Again.
The Third will never get to grow up to be a nerd
With or without the hairy chest
Because the third time was not the charm.

They say Zero's the Hero
And it turns out that one is accurate,
But you don't know until you know.
You certainly wish you could go back to zero,
Before all this grief stole everything from you,
Because life was better when there was none.

Gutted

I built a life for you
A life with you
I picked everything out
And arranged it the way you like
I made our house a home
And filled it with my love
I lovingly made special meals
Ones I hoped you'd eat
I learned to sew your clothes
And made you a special quilt
I studied ways to remove stains
And clean grout
I walked our dogs
The ones we adopted together
I washed your dishes
And your clothes
I put them away
And didn't complain...too much
I tended our garden
In the yard that we loved
I always kissed you goodnight
And told you I love you
I hugged you every chance I got
And wrapped you in my loving spirit

I held your hand when you were ill
Took care of you each day

But now that you're gone
I hate it here
How could you leave me all alone?
I am furious with everyone
How could God take you from me?
I could burn this house to the ground
What did I do to deserve this?
I wasn't perfect enough?
Looking at these walls, these pictures,
I cannot stand the sight
Who thought greige was a nice wall color anyway?
I want to tear it down
In fact, all these walls have to go
I won't stop until there's nothing left
Every wall of every room,
I gutted the kitchen and the baths
Now everything matches how I feel
And I have no regrets.

Brightside

At least they're not in pain anymore.
As if your pain doesn't matter.

You're young, you can always have another!
As if one life can replace another.

At least you have other kids, you should focus on them.
As if your grief is not important.

It could be worse, you could have died too.
As if you don't feel guilty enough.

At least they didn't die.
As if that solves all your problems.

God needed them more.
As if you need another reason to be angry with God.

At least you only lost a leg.
As if you don't have permission to mourn the loss at all.

You should be grateful it's not worse.
As if grief is only acceptable in the most extreme
conditions.

At least you have their memories
As if that is somehow anything close to the same as
having them.

You have to treasure the time you did have with them.
As if you're wrong for wanting, needing, more.

At least it's unlikely to happen with the next one.
As if you care at all about the hypothetical "next one".

You have so many people to support you, just ask.
As if you have the ability to set aside your pain and
organize volunteers.

At least it's over now and you can move forward.
As if grief is a just a rest stop and not a tattoo.

Everyone

Everyone wants to help you
If it fits their schedule
Everyone hopes you'll feel better
As long as you don't talk about it too much

Everyone is waiting to be there for you
If only you would reach out

Everyone will do anything to make it easier for you
As long as they don't have to go out of their way

Everyone would bring you dinner
If they were sure you would like it

Everyone is thinking of you
As long as they can just add you to their prayers

Everyone wants an update
If they can be the first to know

Everyone hopes you find your spark again
As long as it's not too bright, too soon

Everyone is cheering for your recovery

If you don't take too long

Everyone will always support you
As long as you have more good days than bad

Everyone would sit with you
If only they had the time

Everyone is understanding
As long as you're managing your grief according to their
timeline

Inconvenient

I'm sorry that my sadness
Is too uncomfortable to be around.
I really can't turn it off,
I'm not trying to bring you down.

I'm sorry that my tears
Are too plentiful for you to handle.
I really don't want attention,
I didn't realize they'd cause such a scandal.

I'm sorry that my heartache
Is too distressing for you.
I really don't enjoy it either,
But surely this is something that you knew.

I'm sorry that my need for grace
Is too draining on your tolerance.
I really am doing my best,
I wish grief wasn't met with such abhorrence.

I'm sorry that my pain
Is too overwhelming for you to process.
I really need you to be here,
I never meant to cause you stress.

I'm sorry that it's all just too much
Too much
Too much
Too much
For you to see.
I really hide it the best I can,
Please don't abandon me.

Discarded

I had a solid friend group,
Was respected among coworkers, too.

They'd ask me for my advice or thoughts,
And to speak at their presentations,
To volunteer at their events,
To assist in operations.

But that was before The Day,
The day that I lost you.

Now my friends are strangers,
My coworkers scatter in my presence.
My knowledge and experience overlooked,
Because I can't deliver it with my former effervescence.

I haven't been myself,
That, I can admit, is true.

Everyone else continued on,
With work, with joy, with life.
Happiness they didn't share,
To shield me, but, it cut me like a knife.

Though I was trapped in my dark,
I needed bright spots to make it through.

Now that time has dulled my pain,
My seat at the table has been filled.
I'm a stranger in my world,
No longer valuable or skilled.

While my life was paused by grief
I watched my worth devalue.

Every day they checked in less,
I'm the strong friend after all.
Not one text or work request,
No answer when I call.

My calendar continued to empty out,
As everyone else's grew.

I could keep trying,
But is it worth getting my feelings hurt again?
What would be the point?
Were they ever really my friends?

Who could throw a friend away so easily,
And replace them with someone new?

So I soldier on, trying to find where I belong,
But I keep my heart guarded.
Because I've already learned
How effortlessly I am discarded.

Blink

Here one minute and gone the next
We've all heard this sentiment before
But you never really think about it
In terms of human life

But when it happens to you
That's exactly how it feels:
Between heartbeats
From one blink to the next

How can you have something one second
And the next it's just over
You go from everything
To nothing in a breath

There's nothing you can do
Nothing will change this outcome
Had you it all and the next thing you know
It's just...gone.

How do you face the next day
When something you held so precious
Has just been erased from your life
Like a project that wasn't saved before closing

But everyone expects you to keep going
As if that life wasn't so important in their universe
Still, every next day when you wake up
You have to remind yourself of that blink

Here you sit in disbelief
Crushed by the loss anew
And somehow it hurts twice as much
The next time it hits you

Just do the next expected thing
Time heals all wounds
Stay strong my friend
We're always here for you

Each platitude more empty than the next
With no regard for how they make you feel
They mean well, perhaps
But none of it is a comfort

You sit alone, tough surrounded
Drowning on dry land
And all you can even think to do
Is wish you had never blinked.

Regret

We did everything we could, but unfortunately

Nothing you did, or didn't do, caused this

I'm so sorry, but there's no heartbeat

We knew this was possibility

I'm sorry to inform you

It's not the outcome we wanted

I'm afraid that it's worse than we anticipated

We've discovered an unforeseen problem

We understand this is not the news you hoped for

I'm alone with only my anguish
My what-ifs, my could-haves
They consume my every waking thought
All I hear are my should-haves

I should have said "I love you" more often

I should have been more understanding
I should have hugged you one more time
I should have read you every book every night
I should have been more patient
I should have more kind
I should have called you
I should have visited
I should have watched all the episodes of your favorite
show
I really should have said "I love you" more.

My mind haunts me at all hours
My former dreams are now mere silhouettes
Of course I can chase them still, but it's not the same
Because it's just me and my regrets

I regret I didn't show you I loved you more
I regret I couldn't give you a son
I regret I didn't thank you enough
I regret I wasn't around more
I regret I didn't listen carefully
I regret the times I hurt your feelings
I regret I waited to make you proud
I regret I didn't treat you as tenderly as you deserved
I regret I didn't ask for your help
I deeply regret I didn't show you I loved you more.

It's too late for all of these feelings
I'm left holding them with no where to go
There is no reprieve for the mourning
But I truly love you, and hope that now you know.

Salt

In my darkest moment
You were celebrating your brightest
I couldn't find it in me to be happy for you
It felt like salt in my wound

I don't know how to explain
Why it felt so personal
Like God took my baby
And gave him to you

I know that's not how it works
But the mind is a tricky thing
When your son was born the very same day
It felt like salt in my wound.

I watched every happy moment
Every gummy smile that you posted
And wished my baby were here, too
To complete my little family

Envy consumed me
I was obsessed with the unfairness
Every time he hit a milestone
It felt like salt in my wound.

I never wished ill on you
Or didn't want you to have your baby
It all just felt so cruel
Why wasn't I good enough for motherhood?

My grief destroyed my heart and mind
I couldn't handle the smallest disappointments
And even something as simple as burning dinner
Felt like salt in my wound

I know it ruined our friendship all those years ago
And I wish I could do it over
It's easier to stand on this side of the pain
And see things as they were

And I know you would forgive me
You always were a generous soul
But I'm afraid that even that small kindness
Would feel like salt in my wound

I don't know that I could keep watching
As your son does everything mine will never
He's an amazing kid
I know you are proud

But between your forgiveness

And watching your sweet boy grow
My envy and grief are still lurking
Saying this salt in my wound.

Stages

I am angry
I am so, so mad
My heart feels utterly shattered
If desolate was a place, I would be it.

I am shocked to find how few real friends I have,
And I am hurt by the realization.
I am horribly jealous of people how have what I cannot:
A feeling of wholeness, of rightness.

This can't be happening to me
This isn't my real life
Why am I never good enough
I hate everything.

I can't stand to see your happy pictures
I envy your late nights
I would give up sleep forever
If it brought them back.

I boil with rage
At the cruelty I've been dealt
And I feel absolutely nothing
I am an empty shell.

I can't eat, I can't think
I don't even want to move
Why would I bother doing any of that?
What would be the use?

I hate. God, do I hate.
Every decision that brought me to this situation
Every entity in the universe that had a hand in it
Everything burns my heart, my mind, my soul.

There is no more joy for me in this life
Nothing that brings any amount of comfort
When I manage to stop crying for a while
All I feel is exhaustion.

What I wouldn't give for the chance
To relive just one day.
Even a bad day
Would be worth any price.

I found a group of others like me
Who have lost someone so beloved
There is comfort here in the lack of expectations
We accept each other as we are, and welcome all
emotions.

I can't have you back
I can't have what we planned
And sometimes it still feels like I have only ashes
But I am learning slowly that I still have some things.

After all, phoenix rise from ashes.

Unfiltered

If I could tell you how I feel
Without having to worry
About what you'd think of me
What you'd say about me
How you'd treat me after.

If I could tell you how I feel
Without having to wrap it in bow
To be careful with my words
The way I say those words
And if you'd understand them.

If I could tell you how I feel
Without you trying to lessen the impact
By telling me it's ok, it'll get better
Or that someone has it worse
And you would just accept it.

I would tell you that I feel
Worse than I've ever felt before
That I cry myself to sleep every night
Which is fine, since I can't stand to be awake.
I don't care if time goes on, everything feels so pointless.

I would tell you that I feel
Alone and so unloved
Like nothing I do will come out right
Because nothing ever does.
I couldn't even bake a pie.

I would tell you that I feel
Like everyone else has what I want.
Like there's not enough good to go around
And so I am left without.
I stare blankly at walls for hours.

If I could tell you how I feel
And you wouldn't judge, just listen
If you would let me know
My feelings are acceptable
And you still love me no matter what

I would tell you that I feel
Like a loser through and through.
Like the guilt might suffocate me.
And though I'm told it's not my fault
It feels very much like it is.

If I could tell you how I feel
If I could find the words
If I even knew how I feel

If I could figure it out

I would tell you that I feel
Like I might need to get some help.

Grateful

I want to thank you now,
I should have done it before,
For being the one to hold it together,
To pick me up off the floor.

I want to tell you now,
I appreciate you more than you know,
You shouldn't have had to set aside your own grief,
While I acted like I was the only one dealt a blow.

I want to explain to you now,
I know I behaved without reason,
Grief altered my brain chemistry,
And I thank you for weathering that season.

I want to apologize to you now,
For all the times it seemed like I didn't care,
For when I functioned like only my feelings mattered,
I'll always carry that regret, it wasn't at all fair.

I want to beg you now,
Even though I may not deserve it,
Please be patient with me a little longer
I'm getting the help I need, please do not quit.

I cannot thank you enough
For standing by my side
While I asked you to ignore yourself
And instead shore up my landslide.

I cannot tell you enough
How much it means to me that you tried
To help me heal though I wasn't interested,
And instead held me while I cried.

I cannot explain well enough
That I regret a lot of my actions
I understand it created a domino effect
And our relationship felt like series of transactions.

I cannot apologize enough,
For not realizing you were struggling, too,
For being so selfish
That I didn't see the emotional toll on you.

I cannot beg enough
Of your forgiveness
You've already given me so much
Thank you for staying in this.

I appreciate you

I am grateful to and for you
You were my rock when I was barely human
I'm sorry I couldn't be the same for you
I know I wasn't the only one going through it.
You have given me so much grace
And I love you.
From the bottom of all that I am,
Thank you.